Healing Her Whole

Stories of Passion, Restoration and Healing
for the Woman You Love

Aaron J. Mobley, Jr.

WWW.AARONJMOBLEY.COM

DEDICATION

There would literally be no reason or reference for this book except for the love and commitment you have made to me. These words would just be those taken from some illustrations void of power and real effect.

It is because of you that I have been able to persevere through some of the greatest and most challenging of times. As others share in our love and dedication to each other, may you always know and remember one thing. Every word, every sentence, every chapter of this book is written for you.

Happy Birthday, Terrie!

TABLE OF CONTENTS

INTRODUCTION

Simply said, sometimes we wish we thought of the right things to say at the time things occurred. Sometimes we wish we did the right thing at the time it happened. Sometimes we just don't.

It's my prayer that as you read this book that you'll find the healing necessary to love stronger, understand one another better, believe greater and ultimately to experience the best days of your life in the restoration of love.

1

If Only I Were There

"Now the serpent was more subtle than any beast of the field which the Lord God had made. And he said, unto the woman, Yea, hath God said, Ye shall not eat of every tree of the garden?"
Genesis 3:1

On a normal day with hectic schedules, overbearing commitments and a backlog of past hopes it's a miracle that any of us are able to squeeze love into the equation, but it seems like it happens so effortlessly when connected to the right individual. This type of love doesn't necessarily have to be romantic in nature. Love is something that all of us have as an innate function. We were born with it, but there are many factors that arise in love that demonstrate how that love is applied.

The extended and most intimate levels of the idea of love is when it is romantically involved and shared with a part of yourself mirrored in someone else. When I speak of loved mirrored I'm speaking of the type of love that you can see as an extension of yourself. Often times, you hear people speak of how someone completes them, is their better half and sometimes they even call them their twin. It's kind of like sharing the same breath even though sometimes you are miles away from one another.

One of the most difficult pills to swallow is the

idea of somehow and in some way not being able to reciprocate the love that has been shared with you back to the sender. Maybe it's a time issue, lack of energy, space or effort, but whatever it is when you're feelings about that person are sincere, you're not a happy camper when you're not successful in demonstrating as well as it's played out in your heart. I suppose that all of us truly believe that we love at our best. We're the perfect characters in the drama of our life and no one can tell us any different.

I believe that sometimes the show that is ongoing in our hearts isn't as vivid in real life as we might think. We often times get really frustrated when others don't receive it and it's only because what we see as our reality they're seeing it as their everyday dream. They dream of you sharing more love or attention with them, but you're smiling on your lunch break patting yourself on the back thinking that you're the best love they've ever had. Do you see how this can be confusing on both sides?

Coming to the realization that quite possibly

you have not loved at your maximum potential can be a very hard pill to swallow. To even think that someone you care about is not being supplied with what they need for you can be heartbreaking. Especially, if you don't know how to make it better or how to make past mistakes right.

Honestly speaking, there are times when we are just not there. Seemingly we just don't have enough to go around. We all know that this is not the case, but it doesn't change the fact that it's how we feel sometimes. So many things, people and responsibilities arise in life that pull on our love supply. As a result, when it comes down to those we are actually in relationship it might seem extremely hard to display what you really feel towards them and you are desperately hoping that know what you're not able to show.

This brings me to this chapter's background story of the biblical portrayal of Adam and Eve. Adam had existed outside of relationship with another individual like him for a while. He was not used to answering or taking care of himself, because he was taken care of by God. Everything that he could ever want was already there when he was formed. It's not so much that he was a self-sufficient man. It was more like he was a well provided for man whose only assignment was to take care of what he was given. Can you see where I'm going with this? A lot of times it can be expected for men to know what it's like to take care of a woman or to be intuitively sensitive to what it might take to always be there for one. There's a lot of witnesses out there who can attest that most of the time it's a learned behavior that only gets better over time. Especially, in a generation where it's sometimes a rare occasion to see examples of healthy long-lasting relationships.

Before Eve's presentation to Adam his sole responsibility was to take care of his surroundings. God realizes that something was missing in his life. He forms the animals and Adam was given the responsibility of naming them which he did very well. But even with all of his companions it didn't satisfy or fulfill the void of relating to himself in a way that was intimate in nature.

Every man would love to be connected to someone who mirrors what they actually look like inside. It has nothing to do with gender-specific characteristics, it has more to do with the part of themselves that is missing as they look in their current worldview. Check this out! Men look for their missing part as well.

Something in Adam's heart was communicating something that the animals couldn't relate to. It was a sound that wasn't carried in the wind, but was felt in the vibration of his existence and God knew it. I'm not completely sure that Adam ever knew that Eve was a part of him. I do believe that he felt within himself that there was a part of himself that he had not seen yet.

Much of the frustrations in manhood comes from the irritation of not being able to see yourself clearly today as well as you do in the future. It's like you know that it's coming. They've told you that it's coming. But it's not here. It's the NOT HERE part that literally drives men crazy. Seeing yourself has nothing to do with physically viewing your appearance by looking in a mirror. It's about your view of the future and what you are presently able to see as yourself today.

Have you ever been a part of an emotional situation with someone and was literally screaming on the inside "Can they not see me?" This is what a man experiences when they can't touch their internal reality yet. Every day. Every moment. Every year that a dream isn't realized or a vision isn't accomplished. This longing to be seen extends even in a deeper level to the connection men have to those they love.

Wonderfully articulated words don't satisfy that level of frustration. You can encourage men to all end and you'll end up frustrated because the words seemingly are not doing the trick. Why is this? Because it's about natural relation. What we are able to touch today and relate back to ourselves is what brings us peace. "Can I say that I did it? Can I say that they came because of me? Can I say that I achieved what I worked so hard for?" These are the types of questions we hear and desperately sometimes strive to acquire a YES for. We want to be able to put our name on it and stamp it as ours. Call it a cavemen quality, but it's just something that men desire.

So, it's hard to tell what Adam knew about Eve beforehand, but if he was anything like today's man he knew that a part of himself was missing. God sees this and puts him in a deep state of sleep. Nothing was happening externally, but there were tons of things happening inside of him that would bring him in direct contact with what he felt living all the time.

He awakes and says, *"Bone of my bone and flesh of my flesh".* No introductions were necessary. No details had to be given as to who she was. He immediately recognized that it was himself mirrored in shared capacity with someone else. Can you imagine the peace that now erases his frustration as he names her bringing claim not ownership, but claim to her as a part of himself? He calls her Woman simply means that she had "come out of him".

Isn't this the hidden frustration that men feel? Not being able to see what's inside of them become a reality? Well, if that was his frustration it was all over. Because now he was literally able to touch what was a hope and a want before. The Bibles says that*, "they were naked and not ashamed"*.

Losing His Grip

We don't hear about much more of their story than that. We assume that they went along with their lives together sharing and communicating as we would. There are no details given that suggest that they weren't the happy go lucky couple as most are. What we do know is that something changed that would alter the course of their lives forever.

One day for whatever reason Adam was not with Eve. He was not around. He was not watching or listening. Question? If he was there do you think that he would he have known who the serpent was or what his intentions were? Sometimes we assume that he had more insight at this time than Eve did. It's anyone's guess. But the fact remains that he was not in the storyline of this unfolding drama at that time. I think that it's important no point out how extremely cunning the serpent was and how he might've intentionally approached Eve at a time where she was unprotected by her husband.

We can only imagine the difficulty Adam faced as he watched this story unfold in reruns after everything does downhill. Having to relive the guilt of not being there or that something was occurring to their damage during his absence unaware.

This is what men feel when something happens involving someone they love outside of their reach. The playback is the worst. Having to relive it over and over again in your head, wanting and attempting to jump back through time to rescue her and not being able to. You've got to know how terrifying this is for a man that truly loves his lady. There is nothing that you can do and everyone expected you to. Oh yes, you do know that the entire world expects us to know. We must've known and could've stopped it. That's how we hear the audience scold us after misfortune occurs.

Adam was slowly losing his grip on his idea of a perfect reality as many men do when encountered with situations that are somehow beyond their control. What's important to think about is the concept of his original command and how he might have been so focused that he forgot the extension that was also his responsibility.

As a man, I know too well what it's like to be so focused on one thing that you use all of your energy on that and not be aware that something else is happening that you have no clue about. Let's take a closer look at Eve's encounter with a decision that would change the course of humanity forever.

THE COMMUNICATION GAP

"Now the serpent was more subtle than any

beast of the field which the Lord God had made. And he said, unto the woman, Yea, hath God said, Ye shall not eat of every tree of the garden?" ***Genesis 3:1***

So, for the first time I'm asking myself a question. What did Eve hear in the conversation with the serpent that she didn't hear while speaking with her husband? There had to have been more going on that she was relating to other than just the idea of being like God right? The need for communication for men and women are sometimes very different and how it's understood sometimes can be COMPLETELY different.

There was something very convincing in this conversation that caused her to drop her defenses and any guards that she had up. What was Eve not telling Adam that the serpent answered before she had the chance to? Was it something that she wanted, but was unwilling to address? Whatever it was according to the serpents plans she took it hook, line and sinker and then communicated to Adam how good it was. You can say it was her persuasive behavior, gorgeous appearance or the like, but whatever it was Adam received it WILLINGLY. She didn't force him to take it. She didn't stuff it down his throat. He accepted it as a choice.

I'm going to offer another perspective that might relate to some of you. Maybe it wasn't her intention to damage him or their relationship. Maybe she was just trying to HELP! You've got to remember that this was her assignment. Just as Adam had his. Eve had hers. She was called to be his "Help Meet" and sometimes in an attempt to help intentions can become misguided if communication does not occur at the point of decision between one another. Yes, it was a bad decision obviously, but could it be that her intentions were pure? It's extremely easy to look at the result of something and automatically assume that there was some sinister motive involved. Honestly speaking, anyone reading this book has had a bad result from a poor decision that was started from a pure place.

Just as Eve's intention might not have been to get them thrown out of the garden. Let's reevaluate Adam's. Let's not throw him under the bus either.

HIS INTENTION WAS NOT TO BE ABSENT!

There's nothing in my mind that leads me to believe that Adam wanted to be absent or that he voluntarily chose not to be around while Eve had a conversation that would result in the greatest loss that either of them could've imagined. Sometimes it's a great idea to sit back and observe the pattern of the one that you love and ask yourself "Would they have stepped in had he known? What would they have done if they were there?" For most of you who are reading this you already know that the results would never have been what they were if the individual you loved was there and aware.

I want you to think about what I just said. Not just there, but aware. Proximity has nothing to do with "Presence" and a man's awareness of what's happening around him and particularly in the heart of the person he's with. As men we can be in the same room, but a million miles away in our heads attempting to plan the next 1,000 years of our family's lives. The mental projections and plans are endless and at the same time we are so occupied with the present that any thoughts of past failures might send us into a terrible tailspin. With that being said, I'm sure that his intention was not to be absent, but rather I would lend myself to believe that he was attempting to do what he knew to do to take care of his wife.

Even though Adam would play the blame game I'm sure that he knew what he had done wrong. Blame as you know is simply an individual response to a lack of responsibility. He wasn't ready yet. Being ready to accept responsibility is the point where you are forgiving the other party for their hand in something, but more than ever ready to accept the fact that you contributed to the entire situation as well.

With everything that we've discussed so far the

general idea is that Adam and Eve found themselves in a corporate decision that led them astray from the original plan. However it started Adam went along with it and that decision sealed their fate.

I cannot imagine what the conversation was as they were being escorted out of the garden. Adam now has to work hard labor while Eve has to endure the pains of delivery to produce what was supposed to become the world's greatest generations. Everything is now hard and with every drop of sweat Adam had to have remembered the one decision that made all of that possible.

Scriptures don't detail what the conversation was from that point on or how they reconciled what had occurred. We do know that they made the best of it. They continued to remain together and for all instinctive realities they maintained a level of intimacy. The idea behind this chapter is to fully understand that the absence of thought or the absence of presence does not have to result in the loss of commitment. They were together no matter what.

So, what would Adam say to his bride after they were now settled outside of the garden? What would his words be to the woman that he so passionately exclaimed was bone of his bone and flesh of his flesh? Hate was not an option, because to hate her was to literally despise himself. She no matter the situation was his and he was hers.

WHAT HE NEEDS YOU TO KNOW:

- I forgive you and desperately need forgiveness of you.
- It wasn't my intention to be absent when you needed me the most.
- I won't leave you unprotected again.
- I know that you were only trying to help.
- I'll say what you need to hear.
- I'll be more sensitive to what you really want.

The Love Letter

I can remember the very moment that I laid my eyes on you. After waiting for so long and dreaming so intensely, I awoke and there you were. Where did you come from? How did God know? Were a few of the many questions that flooded my heart. It was like I was looking in the mirror and reflecting every prayer, every desire and every passion I had ever felt. It was you that I had been longing for and I didn't even know it. I laugh inside when I think of all of the things I named and claimed as mine trying to fill the void that I felt within.

But as you well know, it was never enough. Something was missing. And that one thing was you.

You didn't need any repairs or additions. You were just how you were created to be. You were made just for me. There's never a day that goes by that I don't look at you and think of myself. How God must love me for bringing you to me. You are God's gift to me.

I took pleasure in guarding you and making sure you knew that it wasn't just about me. It had a lot to do with you. There was no way that I could've made my dreams come true without you. As much as you needed me. I needed you.

It has always been one of my greatest privileges to walk alongside you in the place where God made just for us. Seeing you live without a care in the world was great peace to me. Knowing that I was there to protect you from harm was like a badge of honor to me. I was one of my greatest achievements.

But as it would happen. One day I wasn't there. Even writing this brings back the memories of that day. The moment I realized what I could've done, what I could've said, how I could've responded. But it was too late. I wasn't there for you.

I didn't stand up in the way that I could've. I didn't reaffirm who you were, who we were together and how we could've overcome. I didn't remind you how complete you were and how nothing needed to be different for me to love you anymore that I already had.

The fact that in some way I wasn't there for you pains me in ways that you will never realize. I should've been there for you as you have always been there for me.

I can't begin to tell you the journals that I have written in my head, the rehearsed defenses, and the many words I would have said if only I were there that day.

I've watched you suffer, cry and grieve the loss of the life we knew before it all seemed to crumble away. But I want you to know that as much I forgive you, I long even more to be forgiven of you. I should've seen it before it happened or sensed what you needed inside. I didn't. But from this moment on I'm watching you. I dedicate the rest of my life to making sure that your heart beats peacefully in peace as we live the rest of our lives together.

2

Standing By You

"..... But while he thought on these things, behold, the angel of the Lord appeared unto him in a dream, saying, Joseph, thou son of David, fear not to take unto thee Mary thy wife: for that which is conceived in her is of the Holy Ghost. And she shall bring forth a son, and thou shalt call his name."

Matthew 1: 18-25

There are a few occasions in life where you have the opportunity to actually display true support to someone that you love. I'm not just speaking of those occasions where there are tons of other people cheering the person on, but more like the times where it's maybe just you and them. Those are the times where true love relationships are defined and a clear stance is taken to stand with them no matter what. It's even more powerful because sometimes we honestly don't think that there is anyone who would. Who would stand with me during this type of situation? That's what's normally said within the heart of a person experiencing deep levels of shame. They don't even expect it and have already decided in their minds that they'll have to go this one alone. But love has a way of pressing through the guard that we sometimes put up in the quest to protect ourselves from further damage.

It takes some real gusto to stand outside of the crowd or the general consensus and say "It doesn't matter what they've done or what it looks like, I'm standing with them". Anyone can stand with a person that everyone loves, but not too many can put up with the accusations that come towards someone that people despise.

The idea behind this level of support is to accurately clarify what love really is. Oh yes, I think everyone thinks that they know what love is, but not too many of us are actually able to walk through the challenge that certifies our love towards others. It would be amazing if we could simply love without challenge or difficulty, but honestly that's not the way it is.

ENCOURAGEMENT AND SUPPORT

There's a difference between Encouragement and Support. Encouragement can be anything used to make someone want to continue doing a certain thing or being a particular way. Actually, many of us are great encouragers. We send cards, emails, phone calls and sometimes even pay special visits to those that we love. That's some great encouragement right there. On the other hand, Support is encouragement that actually shows up to help them do whatever you are promoting in their lives. Support is like encouragement on steroids.

Life has a way sometimes of throwing all of us into a situation where encouragement is absolutely appreciated and valued, but the support of those who love us is what actually sustains us through the roughest times of our lives. I think sometimes that when given the opportunity to support it must be understood that just maybe the person needing it had no idea that they would need it. It's very easy to assume within ourselves that they should have known better or seen it coming. If that were the case many of us would be unsupported right now. Because I can almost guarantee that there have been some situations that you did not ever think that you would be in and that you are very grateful to have had true support with you every step of the way.

A PERFECT SETUP

It is amazing to me how divinely orchestrated the Lord's plans are for our lives. It's like He sets the stage, gets all of the players in place, sells the tickets, opens the show and here we are walking on the stage and have no clue that the show has started and we are the main act.

It seems like the story of Joseph and Mary is just like that. Isn't it interesting to you that God did not choose a virgin that was just single. He specifically chose someone who was already connected to an individual. Some of you already know where this is going. Before the situation ever arrived God gave Mary a pillar of support, but I'm sure that Joseph had no knew what he was signing up for. He had probably seen many others get married and have a normal family and live the rest of their lives doing what families did at that time. He didn't know that the girl that he was engaged to would give birth to the savior of the world. Who would have thought such a thing? He approached this situation as he was taught, following all of the customs that were normal for that day. Even though, they had not been intimate Mary was his. They had a commitment already and he was planning on seeing it finalized.

In this same fashion, it is impossible to gauge the cost that any of us will have to pay for supporting the people that we love. The price many times is very costly and many choose not to continue because of it. How do you maintain who you are when others are tearing down who you love? What do you say to them when their words seem justified? In the absence of a logical explanation it's always good to let love speak. Love always has the perfect response in situations that seem utterly confusing not only to others, but mainly to you.

Joseph had no clue what he was in for and the role that his life would play in benefiting the entire world. It was the perfect setup.

IT'S SHOWTIME

The same way this was divinely orchestrated we have to know that whenever God allows us to be connected to love in relationship that it is not by some happenstance or coincidence. He already knows that you have what it takes to support that individual through the greatest of storms and tests.

What was it in Joseph's character that made him so fit to carry this level of responsibility? We understand that his bloodline was a qualifying factor, but there had to have been something more about him as a person that proved that he was the one. If anyone else was chosen they might have taken the first opportunity to run for the hills. This was not the case. He made a choice to stay.

Making the choice to stay during difficult seasons is not as easy as some would think. The difficulty is not about whether you're going to leave. That's already settled. You're staying and you want to. The issue is how to handle the situation that is causing your love to be challenged by such great lengths.

I honestly believe that every man that stands by the woman he loves has this "thing". I'm not sure what to call it actually, but it's something that makes them airtight. Their love doesn't escape and the contaminants to it can't come in. They've got that thing. Joseph had it and

God knew it. God knew that Joseph wouldn't leave her. Do you think that he would have chosen a man who would?

There is something about your love relationship today that God is assured will stand the test of time. Why? Because he knows who the players are. He's vetted you both. He's gone through your history and he knows your background. Yes, there'll be times of great disappointment and challenge, but you've got that "thing" and God knows it.

THE BIG ANNOUNCEMENT

As shocking as it was for Joseph accept you have to remember that Mary was as shocked as he was and more so. It was not just about the divinity involved, but also the repercussions that would occur when others found out about it. No one would believe her, they would laugh at her in the streets, call her a whore, untrustworthy, a loose woman and the like. They would throw dirt on her commitment to Joseph. They might attempt to punish her and very likely kill her. All of these things were very strong possibilities. It was just not safe for her to be a part of any of this.

I can only assume what the conversation was like between her and the man that she loved. Having to explain what had occurred and the strange conversation she had with the angel. I'm sure that his face displayed utter disbelief that he was married to someone that would tell him such things. How do you convince someone that what appears to be unfaithfulness really isn't when everything looks like it?

Even though we are discussing one of the greatest stories of love and compassion in history, we all know that there are some stories that we live that are not so illustrious. We didn't see an angel or hear a voice from heaven say anything. We simply found ourselves carrying a situation that we were not proud of. Under normal circumstances Mary could've probably started running down the streets, screaming excitedly that she was carrying her husband's son. This was not one of those times.

She rather had to in fear anxiously share the news of what was happening in her life.

I want to take a moment to acknowledge the difficulty that sometimes woman experience when sharing not so good news with the one they love. The idea of something causing a separation from their lover, protector and friend can be absolutely disheartening. Can you imagine how intensified this was in the culture of Mary's day? Even though this was good news it certainly didn't look like it to anyone else.

Some of you reading this are having to relive the moment that you had to share some unfortunate news. The thoughts that went through your mind as you prepared to speak what you didn't even want to think must have been the worst times of your life. But it was in these situations that a clarity came in your heart concerning the person that you were so passionate about being with. You either realized that their commitment towards you and your well-being was real or you realized that it was only a mirage for what they actually felt.

I believe that it's in situations like this that the nature of love is actually seen. Even though at first it might not seem so grand in display. Joseph didn't throw her a party or go run to tell his friends. It wouldn't have been rational, but he did make a step in the right direction out of his heart of love. The scriptures make a point of telling us that Joseph was a "just" man. He wasn't willing to publically embarrass her, but chose rather to protect her and put her away privately. This might sound like the opposite of love, but all of us can see that something was in his heart growing towards another option.

Sometimes we can neglect to see the heart of an individual when it is not demonstrated in the way that we may be accustomed to or the way we expect. You could not have expected Joseph to respond some other way. This was the strangest thing that he had ever heard and it would definitely take divine intervention for him to understand another way.

What Joseph was being asked to support

happened without his knowledge, without him being privy to the conversation and without him having the ability to ask the angel some questions of his own. You've got to know how frustrating and confusing this might have been for him. The only option that he was being given was to trust the words of the woman he loved and go along with the program.

SPACE TO LOVE

Giving the individuals you love the space to understand is one of the greatest gifts that you can give. Yes, they love you. Yes, they value you. Yes, they want to be with you. Those are not the points of contention. It is the understanding of how they can support you is sometimes the puzzle. When it's all settled you've got to remind yourself that they want to support you and sometimes it's not a love thing. It's a how thing.

As it would turn out, God saw his heart and knew that he had the ability to make sense out of a senseless situation. God communicates with him the sincerity of what Mary had shared and gives him the support and guidance he needs to support and guide her.

Look at this. It wasn't that he couldn't. It was that he just didn't know how. He now has what he needs to stand by her willingly.

WHAT HE NEEDS YOU TO KNOW:

- I've made the choice to support you.
- I refuse to allow my love to be silent.
- I'm not running or hiding. I'm willing to be public with my support.
- You don't have to be afraid of sharing what you feel might hurt me. I won't run.
- It's sometimes not a love thing. I'm honestly searching to discover how.
- Give me the opportunity to love you the way you deserve to be loved.
- I'm standing with you no matter what.

Only God could have made this possible. Only a being so mysterious yet so powerful and true could have made this day become, as real as me and you; a day when I declare to the world, despite all adversity, my unwavering decision to love you and be by your side for the rest of my life. I can imagine how this letter might catch you off guard. In your mind I know you've battled between how to accept God's will and help me to understand at the same time.

It's taken my some time to accept the reality of what's happening inside of you. In a normal world under normal circumstances this type of thing would be a man's dream. But the uncommon thing that you're experiencing honestly resulted in the exact opposite for me. It became my greatest nightmare. I've taken some time to think and reflect on who I have known you to be. An honorable woman of powerful truth could never lie about a gift so holy and true. The beauty that has drawn me to your side time and time again has shown me something that I don't know how to contain. So beloved, please hear these simple words from my heart to you.

Today I write to reassure you, my loving angel, of my unyielding choice to face my greatest fear - the terrifying thought of losing you to the misunderstandings of my own heart. I originally assumed the worst, because it was the only thing that I knew. But as God would have it. He showed me you.

The forces that fight against our love daily seem to be far beyond what our eyes can simply see, but I'm thankful that our Father has created such love in our hearts, and that love will in turn prove to be the only anchor that will keep us planted as we await the joy that will one day fill our lives and the world.

True love ignores every opposition anywhere it can be found, including this seeming obstacle to the sweet advancement of our love. So, I stand this day and say to you, that for your love I will do anything... for your love I will go anywhere... for you, my love, I will face any situation or circumstance no matter how contrary it may seem. For you I will stand!

There is not a man that I won't fight for you! There's no army that I won't run through. I will use all of my strength and honor to make sure that you are able to live in the joy of our love forever.

Yes, I've seen how the Eyes of people, near and far away, stare piercingly at you with great scorn every time you walk by, for your kindness they return with turned up noses the minute you look away and pass by. I sense their deep resentment, their harsh words I hear... I've watched as they even look you straight in the eyes with judgments so obvious any person could read them from miles away.

For me, I might as well be stoned dead in an open place rather than watch helplessly as, humiliated, I am defamed beyond imaginations. The mockery of toddlers, a sly word from the women around the corner, at the town square and even among my own I have become the latest outcast in the sight of those I once held dear; my dignity recklessly dragged through the mud of shame.

However, this one thing I do; standing strong and relentless, I take every single stroke and blow in my stride, if only that it would stay away their prejudice and keep you, my darling, from harm and ridicule. I'll do it all over again for the one reason in this world which matters so dearly to my heart – you!

The depth of my love and commitment to you will keep me, forever standing - an immovable shield, now and beyond, pushing away every deadly public opinion regarding this truly unspeakable yet undeniably wonderful gift forming within you.

A most miraculous manifestation indeed, for God has revealed to me in a dream that truly you are exempted from every offense launched against you. He has shown me unto me his defense and protection of you. It's a love that I cannot deny, for I too hold it true.

In all actuality, the punishment they present would be acceptable. But I now realize that what's happening to you is above what man can ever really understand. They don't know you like I do. So, even though there are many that might not understand why I stand with you so strong, I don't care. I have made my choice and that choice is you.

For you, I will go the extra mile… for you I will forever stand. No matter what, I will forever stand by your side. Through the hardships of isolation, the despair of uncertainty and the agony of watching you hurt. But I would do it a million times over because of one powerful truth…. . Because I love you.

3

Getting You Back

"…… Therefore it shall come to pass, when the Egyptians shall see thee, that they shall say, this [is] his wife: and they will kill me, but they will save thee alive."

Genesis 12:10-20

Decisions, decisions, decisions. That's how all life-altering scenarios start. Whether they end with smiles or sadness they all begin with a decision. Often times, it's just one decision that leads to a series of events that were once controlled but are now the exact opposite.

I love to think that today's decisions are based solely on the information that we have available. Contrary to popular opinion, I don't think that people are just out there just deciding to make a decision that will ultimately turn out terrible. At least I choose not to think of it that way. I honestly believe that we chose the best route based on what we know about ourselves, others and the particular situation.

There's certainly some guilt all of us feel when our best-laid plans turn out to be some of the most life-threatening ones and overcoming that guilt sometimes takes lots of love, loads of forgiveness and unfortunately sometimes many years. It's amazing how a good idea can turn out so bad. Such as was the story of Abraham and Sarah at this time in history.

Their story is an amazing one that begins with them undertaking this vast journey towards a place that they had never heard about or even imagined. Things were going very well where they were. Even though Sarai had not given Abram any children they still maintained a sense of normalcy and happiness. Their future was still bright.

Abraham now hears the Lords voice instruct him to do something that was probably the weirdest thing him or his family could have ever imagined. He most certainly would've shared it with them and as families behave they might've laughed him to scorn. They would not have heard of this God that he spoke of or the things that this God instructed him to do.

Fearlessly, he made his way being separated from everything that he had known. Everything that was familiar and common. He leaves it all for something he could not even see. Remember this idea because this is the essence of what we'll share in this chapter.

CLEAVING AND LEAVING

Leaving home for the first time for most of us is a really big deal. It's filled with a variety of emotions from happiness to sadness, to anxiety and maybe fear. But the rewards of such decisions are those that override all of them. Despite the feelings, we see something that is appealing ahead. We might not know what it is or just how it's all going to be accomplished, but step by step we have confidence that it will.

All of us at some point in our lives will have to make a choice to do what I like to call the "Leave and Cleave". It's derived from Genesis's instruction on what should be demonstrated when a man discovers his wife. Scriptures says it like this in Genesis 2:24-25, *"therefore shall a man leave his father and his mother and shall cleave unto his wife: and they shall be one flesh. And they were both naked, the man and his wife and were not ashamed."*

The assumption here is that there is an automatic function that should be activated in the heart of a man when he commits to his wife. He has now found his "good thing". He now makes the willing choice to leave what has produced him to cleave to what he feels has come out of him and mirrors his heart. This is the person that I'm willing to leave everyone for is the sentiments that are normally heard.

As the story of Abraham and Sarah continues to develop, they both encounter a situation where this premise will be challenged to its greatest limits.

Isn't amazing how situations can literally shake the foundation of a decision? There's nowhere to run and no way to get back there. You just have to accept the fact that you've made a decision while praying to God for a way out.

A FEAR MOVE

Fear is a terrible thing that most of the times stems from the thought of losing something. It might be a car, relationship, money, house, health, happiness or anything, but the fear of losing those things results sometimes in crazy decisions that aren't well thought through. Honestly speaking, in the absence of fear we probably would not have made any of the decisions that we made during that time.

Having to live with a bad decision can cause a lingering pain that people just don't understand. You're dealing with the present and attempting to move ahead, but the memories of what you allowed to occur are still haunting you during times that you should be shouting for joy. You've made progress, but are still looking at that one decision that would've seemingly pushed you that much farther ahead.

Abraham is faced with a terrible dilemma as he attempts to help his family during the famine being experienced in Canaan. He makes the decision to go to Egypt to seek assistance, but there was only one problem with this plan. Sarah is beautiful. So, Abraham decides to pass her off as his sister instead of his wife. He becomes fearful that he would be killed so that she could be taken from him.

I want you to remember something. Abraham had left everything to pursue this great future. It had taken all of the faith he had to do it and the thought of now losing who he was and who he left with was unbearable. He had to make a choice and a plan.

What I would like for you to understand behind this story is that Abraham was in fear. He was afraid that because of this situation he would lose something. I'm sure that he was also afraid about what would happen to her in the custody of someone else, but it was his life that he was almost sure would be lost. He had heard of the stories of situations just like his and he didn't want to be the next statistic.

For most men, it's a complicated act to communicate they are afraid. The idea that we're looked to for so much strength and poise is sometimes what distracts us from sharing what might really be our reality. So, yes. There are situations where we have no answers, no resources, no assistance and clue as to what to do next. In addition to this, we have the beauty of the one we love staring at us every day believing that we already have the plan that we know we don't. So, in our silence please understand that there just might be some fear hiding behind our strong stance.

Every man wants to hold fast the trust of the one he loves. He wants to be assured that you know that he's doing what he can to ensure that you are secure. And then when there are times when things happen to fall apart. He wants to know that you trust him to put it all together again.

Most bad decisions that men make towards the one they love are in close relation to some level of fear. This fear is demonstrated in many ways. It can be in pushing away the person they love or simply making a series of bad decisions that result in their loss.

As the story continues, Abraham's decision does not go as well as planned. Sarah is still taken from him. Despite the well-laid plan he is now separated from the one person who is directly connected with his promise. What he feared the most has happened and he is still alive watching in living color. What agony this was for him? If he was dead he would not have to see her carried away like a purchase in the market. He wouldn't have to envision her behind the walls of Pharaoh's palace. But he wasn't dead. He was very much alive watching his worst fears realized.

We can all imagine the utter disappointment Abraham felt in himself as he watched her be taken away. The replay that went on in his head as he thought of what he could've done differently to change those course of events. It's the picture show that never changes. You can't go back, but desperately want to do whatever you can to regain her trust in you again. You want her to know how sorry you are for putting her through, but she can't hear you. The only thing that you could hope for is that in her heart she knows that you're fighting every day to get it all back.

It's hard to watch your decisions cause the

person that you love suffer. It's painful to think that just maybe if you had taken a little more time to think or if you had planned a little better that things would be different.

Sarah trusted Abraham not only as her husband, but also as her spiritual guide. She honestly probably thought that the plan would work because he said so. Can you see how her trust in him could have been tainted as she is carried away and for some time disconnected from the security she once knew? But what I love about this story is that God gives Abraham a chance to regain her trust and win her back. He intervenes through a series of events with Pharaoh which reveal her true identity resulting in her release. Abraham finally has her back.

Now here's where it gets interesting. Sarah has to forgive Abraham. She can't hold onto what he allowed to happen to her. Maybe should would have rather he had a duel to the death, but that wasn't what he chose. She had to forgive.

Some people have been hurt in relationship do not wish or try to forgive in any way, shape or form. The result is that it causes you to suffer the pain of the experience forever. If forgiveness is not welcomed it might be the loss of peace for the rest of your lives. Everyone knows that we don't forgive for others only. We forgive for ourselves. It wasn't God's intention that Sarah continued this journey holding this against Abraham. She had to accept the fact that in the middle of a good plan it turned bad.

The story ends as Abraham gets her back in his loving embrace again. I can imagine how he wiped off the makeup that the Egyptians wore at that time. How he gave her the clothes that they had taken from her and how he reconnected her with the purpose that had called them away. Wow! What an amazing journey love is especially when you are able to get back what might have been lost forever.

WHAT HE NEEDS YOU TO KNOW:

- I know things didn't go as planned.
- I need your forgiveness.

- I didn't mean to put you and what we built in harm's way.
- I admit that my decision was because I might have been afraid.
- I am working hard to regain your trust.
- I'm doing what I can to give you back everything you've lost.
- I'm never letting you go again.

The Love Letter

You are the light of my whole life, the joy of my heart… the essence of my being. The years we've spent together should be etched in stones that would last forever, never to age in the memory of our love.

I can't imagine what it would feel like to not be with you. I'm not sure that there could be anyone who would make me stop fighting for you. It never crossed my mind that anyone would even attempt to remove you from the place I hold so dear. The thought of someone challenging the union that we have made before God is shocking. It's current reality while astounding makes me want you more and more. To know what is mine and that another seeks to have it is unacceptable. No, no one can separate you from me, my love. No one has been given such right to come between our love and devotion, because truly you and I were meant to be!

I know beloved that my actions that day led me to losing you in the first place, but it was solely in an attempt to keep hope alive the best way that I knew how. There's one thing that I'm absolutely certain of. This is that no matter what the situation is or how far you are away from me, as long as I'm alive, my eventual joy of getting you back will forever remain my reality.

I reassure you my love, that as long as I'm alive, no mountain, no ocean, no seas; no matter how deep or stormy, no lakes, no stream or valleys, not even the hottest desert can stop me from taking back that which is rightfully mine, for out of a momentary loss of heart; call it fear or doubt, I lost my love to the hands of another. Up until this very moment, as you're not in my arms yet again, my heart burns like wild forest fires because of your absence, the loneliness consumes me; killing me slowly but killing me indeed. The sheer notion of losing you delivers a jagged edged shaft directly to my already bleeding heart.

Daily I fight with everything I have to gain an advantage to win you again. It's harder than the first time I laid eyes on you. Then I only had a glimpse of what a life would be like with you. Now, I have tested the depths of your love. The power of your beauty and the grace of your light. I've made your face my mirror and the love of your life my sustaining joy.

Daily every second without you feels like days without end... constantly, I think about on the terrible effect it would have on our lives if you ever ended up lost forever all because of my own weakness, especially against your own will. I would never forgive myself for my weakness in defending you.

But now, you will never know the joy floods my

soul as I finally am within grasps of having you to myself once again! But this time, forever! What I once lost is now, at last, restored to me! How much brighter the day seems now that you are once again a full part of it. Now, did I just say '... a part of it'? No! You make each and every day of my life. You make every moment exactly what it is – a testimony of our sweet divine love. I am glad to have you in my arms again.

Our entire journey this far is evidence of God's loving grace over our lives, being the sole architect of our love. Isn't it amazing How our God handled everything and person that had taken our love hostage and held it for ransom? But now, the oppressor has been oppressed and my sunshine is fully restored to her true place of joy, happiness, peace and lasting love – in my arms, at last!

Oh, will you ever forgive me, my sweetness for putting you through such an ordeal? Will you ever again trust this undying love I have for you? Oh, love, I promise to never again let you out of my sights. Never again will this be... never again will I lose you. I'll fight forever if I ever have to, that I may keep you forever safe and happy. Unconditionally yours... Forever

4

I Won't Waste It

"And behold, a woman in the city which was a sinner, when she knew that Jesus sat at meat in the Pharisees house, brought an Alabaster box of ointment... "
Luke 7:37

Everyone wants to be loved. I don't care how much individuals declare that they don't need it that's a lie. In some way, shape or form we all do. There's something within us that no matter how successful we are or how busy we are we still long for someone to see our value and respond with their love. Unfortunately, sometimes there are those that honestly are not sure whether they will ever discover what it feels like to actually experience this.

Maybe it's because of the time that has gone by or because of several failed attempts to connect to love. The reality is that there are many who have just given up. It would appear as though everyone is looking for something to benefit them instead of even looking for way to make you happy.

The pursuit for mutually benefiting relationships can be very tiresome. Looking for individuals that you can love and that will love you sometimes are few and far in-between. It's not just love that you're looking for actually. It's value.

It's a hilarious thought, but sometimes all of us like to be fought for and possibly over. It's the idea that there is something that someone sees in me that they're willing to go against someone or something for. No one wants to be seen as an expendable item that can be easily replaced. We all would rather have a golden like gift status in the lives of those we love and care for.

Seeing the value in an individual goes beyond their appearance or what they can do for you. It reaches much deeper than that. When you truly value someone it says that you are able to identify them based not on their outward appearance (that is subject to change), but rather their internal treasure. You see the benefit they offer not only to you, but also to the world and you desire to protect and promote it.

A treasure is most of the times hidden in some of the darkest and dirtiest of places. Not only is it hid, but it's usually forgotten about. Isn't it amazing how some of the world's greatest treasures are right underneath the surface, but not too many people are willing to dig for it.

I often think about the illustration of the baby Jesus as he is in a place where no one would've ever imagined that a king would be born. He wasn't in a palace surrounded by thousands of servants. He was born in a stable. This is not where people would've expected a king to be born. But he was.

Isn't it amazing how some of the greatest gifts to mankind can come from some of the lowliest of beginnings? But what's remarkable about this is that even though he was there his gift to the world was still intact.

Sometimes it's very easy to look at others with a qualifying view. You've already sized them up and predicted how effective their lives will be and what they'll be able to add to yours. You've placed them in your unimportant category and you've now moved your attention to those who you feel as though can add a little more of what you're looking for. Some of the most divine packages have been looked over based on their presentation just like that.

In spite of his current surroundings and birthplace there were people who were looking for him. They didn't care where he was or how he looked. They needed to find him. The idea behind having a heart for love is to fully accept the fact that no matter where you have come from in life that God has someone looking for you. It's not about how qualifying your life has been to the status quo. They're not concerned about that at all. They're looking for you.

The stars were attracting the Wise Men to Jesus just as he was at that time. He didn't have time to get ready or get a custom made robe. They weren't coming for the appearance of him having everything together according to what the eyes could see. They were coming for the value inside of him. What's absolutely phenomenal is that he was a baby. He wasn't even full grown. His kingdom wasn't announced and he didn't have any fans. Yet they saw him for who he was.

This is the same predicament that this woman finds herself in during this chapter's story. She wasn't popular to the crowd and to others didn't have anything to offer Jesus. But she did. She had herself.

One of the hardest things for a person to accept

when their life's story isn't as beautiful is the understanding that someone is going to love them for who they are. Especially when they are used to people using them for only what they could offer or do for them at the time.

How irritating is it for you when you only get phone calls when someone needs something or when there's some emergency that they need to be rescued from? It's kind of frustrating isn't it? You would honestly just appreciate a phone call where the caller on the other end just says, "Hey, I was just calling to tell you I love you", "Just calling to check on you" or "I was just calling to hear your voice". The bottom line is that everyone wants to feel valued. Whatever feelings this woman felt she musters up enough courage to go where Jesus was.

It takes superhuman strength sometimes to overcome some of the challenges that befall us. But just think about what it was like for a woman in those days. Not only did she have to be the perfection of purity, if her life was anything opposite she was not only scorned, but punished in some of the harshest of ways. Look at the determination in the heart of this gift.

She finds herself having to make a difficult decision. The decision was to either stay where she was or go "as she was" to have an encounter with the one person that could change her life forever. The remarkable lesson in this passage is that she was strong enough to handle the background noise. She didn't crumble at the looks of those that despised her or at the opinions of others. She stood tall and presented herself as a gift. Unashamedly she went bearing the best gift she had and was accepted full heartedly. Not for what she brought, but for who she was.

Ladies, the person God has sent or the one that's on the way doesn't have this fantasy of what you might be. They're looking for something far deeper than that. It's not about the perfect person, but honestly more about the perfect passion. A man loves a woman that has a passion about herself and her value. Even if sometimes in the past she did possess any of those things. What's important to him is that you have it now.

Guess what? He didn't waste it. He didn't do as others did as she encountered men in her past. They used and abused her beauty, took from her the most precious things to her and left her possibly in a more damaged place. He didn't waste it. Everything she presented he accepted and welcomed. Her tears were as valuable to him as the oil was that she used to anoint him.

The one who God sends to love and restore you will value every part of who God has created you to be. You won't have to pick and choose which parts to present. You'll be able to be vulnerable exposing your weaknesses and flaws and still receive the love and care as if they weren't there at all.

It's important to always recognize the acceptance of the one who loves you. The value they see in you and the heart in which they receive your gifts. It's really not important to him where you've been or how tainted your past was. He sees you for who you are. Don't push him back. He's there waiting on you. He won't waste it.

WHAT HE NEEDS YOU TO KNOW:

- You don't have to pretend that you're perfect.
- Don't be afraid to bring the best of yourself to me.
- I see you as you are and not what others expect you to be.
- I appreciate your courage. I know what it took for you to love me.
- You're gifts and treasure are safe with me.

Let me begin by telling that I realize how much it has taken for you to come to me. It's honestly taken more for you than it has for others. In light of what you've been through, the words that you've heard spoken to hurt you and the actions of others, I know it's been a lot. I want you to know that I've always watched you. Waiting on this very moment. The day that you would finally give my love a chance.

There is no question that your steps today to show me your heart are real and pure. Others may be second guessing the time that I've taken with you, but I really don't care. It's for moments just like this for which I'm really here.

Hopefully, you have seen that it is because of my sacrifice of love for you that I have chosen to take the path that I have. I've been willing to suffer and bear the tremendous marks of this journey to only arrive to this day where I'll show you what love really is.

I'm sure that others have tried to fill the voids in your heart. They've made promises and guarantees that they were never intent of carrying out. But beloved love of mine, I today will make you a promise that will follow you for all eternity. The power of my love and dedication will never fade away.

Therefore, I say to you this day: I will not waste it!

I will not waste the good gifts you bring me, the actions produced from your heart of love, your heartfelt sacrifices and your diligent strides towards me will all pay off. I will not allow your great kindness which you have given from the depth of love and which has cost you so much go to nothing.

How much boldness it had to have taken for you to come to me. How much thought you must've undertaken to weigh the risks of approaching me surrounded by so many doubters, but you came. You came to me when others called you crazy. When they mocked you as you gave your best without ever considering that it was probably your last.

Oh my precious gift, that's what I call you. For your love towards me has made what I have been called to do so much worth the pain. To see the smile on your face every day from this moment on is why I came.

Keep giving it your all my dear, your gifts are safe with me. I will not waste it.

Eternally Yours!

5

"And Miriam and Aaron spoke against Moses, because of the Ethiopian woman, whom he had married: for he had married an Ethiopian woman."
Numbers 11:1

As statistics would have it there are many who ever find real love. They go peacefully or angrily into eternal sleep never knowing what it is to be loved by another in the most intimate of ways. The thought of this is disappointing for some, but the idea of having your love stolen because of the feelings of others are far more terrifying.

The fact of the matter is that we love who we love. Something about them just makes our idea of the future amazing. We can't even imagine what life would be like without them. But as life would have it there are others who don't see the value sometimes in who we choose.

In the previous chapter, there were men who boldly confronted Jesus concerning the woman that he accepted and loved. They actually scolded him for allowing her not only to come into his presence, but also the idea that this type of woman was touching him.

Isn't it amazing that the crowd was not who she was coming for? She wasn't coming for them and probably didn't even look them in the eye. They weren't her goal. She was coming for him. Sometimes the noise from the crowd is only, because you didn't come for them.

Having the need to have your loved approved by the majority can be a tricky game that might just result in you losing what you actually want. It's not about choosing based on what they want, but rather what you know you need.

The backdrop of this chapter's story is exotic and extremely interesting. Moses chooses a woman that went against everything that his family had ever known. She didn't come from their town or speak their language, but something in her aroused a desire within him.

Can you imagine what they must have put her though? Or possibly the cold shoulders she experienced as she walked by? Remember. This was a foreigner and a stranger to their customs and beliefs. As much as she loved Moses she also needed them to feel secure in this place so far away from home. Even though their arguments and complaints were loud it couldn't stop him from marrying her. Moses made a decision to love.

Some of you reading this have made some of these same types of decisions. Having to choose between loving the one you're with or retreating to the sidelines because of the retaliation from those you thought had your best interest in heart. I've got to be honest. Not all advice is bad advice. Sometimes it's given from a pure place. But it's still your choice. The life you live in love must be carried out through your own intentions to embrace it.

I believe what most woman want and what anyone wants for that matter is to know that even if others object that they'll still be chosen. Even if the world argues against your decision that you'll still choose to continue the plans that you've made with them.

Moses could have backed up on his commitment because of his families objections. Honestly, they had known him much longer and probably felt like they knew what was best for him. They probably already had their pick and made the arrangements. But he stood strong to what he committed in his heart.

What a powerful statement this is to love in spite of what others are saying. To put your heart in the hands of your chosen regardless of the backlash that you might experience. Only you know what mirrors you heart and what will satisfy the dreams that others have no clue are even there.

WHAT HE NEEDS YOU TO KNOW:

- I'm not listening to what others might say or think about you.
- I see what others can't.
- I'm going to honor my commitment to you and our love.
- You are my priority and I will always honor you as that.
- I'll defend my choice in you always.

What words fair enough would there ever be to describe you, my love? What better way would there be to define clearly enough my insatiable love for you? What worthy act would it be that might be proved great or powerful enough to portray my undying commitment and admiration for you?

No height, no depth nor space could express how much I love you.

My heart beats in resounding rhythm of your name every second that I breathe, every time I look in your eyes I see my only reason for gracing the face of this earth – you. Yes, it's for God I live, but my heart it's for you that I love.

Sweetheart, many others might disapprove of

our love, they may fight scrape or scratch for all I care; they can turn up their noses and roll over on the floor if need be, but nothing can deter the love that I have for you. There are some things in life that's simply unexplainable and for some our love maybe. But it's of no consequence to me. It's just the reality of what our love has chosen to be.

I have grown to love you in ways that sometimes I can't understand. Sometimes I just sit picturing our sweet tender moments together in my mind's eye, realizing that all I want is to hold you eternally warm in the tender loving embrace of my arms.

Your love awaits you darling, your knight in shining armor runs to your rescue. No they can't stop you! They can't stop you from enjoying the beautiful gift of love that you have in me. Truthfully, you aren't like what others may have expected. You don't fit the idea that others may have had for me. But I don't care. You have proven to me this moment's greatest creation to me.

The world may say no... they can bring down mountains and create bottomless valleys, but they can't decide for me who to love and who to take as my own. So, I boldly, unequivocally choose you!

Despite all the negative gestures from our friends and family, regardless of our futile efforts to meet halfway just to prove to them that what we share is real, they still persist in trying to tear us apart. But they forget that which the bible had said, that love conquers all.

Our love, my dear, shall by far overcome every challenge that stare us in the face. So, don't ever worry about changing beauty for me or anyone else. It's your difference that caught my attention. Your willingness to present me the best that you had to offer and I chose out of many others the gift that I never thought I could have.

Would it be fair to forfeit such a love unhinged as ours? A love so selfless, so warm, so strong? How disgraceful would I If I let you go simply because of what others may say, think or do? As far as I remain, my only choice is YOU!

You mean the world to me. No one else could've packaged my desires and wants in such a beautiful gift as you. Why would I care what they say? Let them talk. I love you sweetheart and that's all that matters to me right now and forever.

I know that God will always defend our love and my choice for you. It's only by a power so divine that we have seen our love contend with the greatest and they all have fallen to the decision I have made for you.

I Love you more than anyone can see or explain. More than these few words can ever really tell. It's for you that I declare to the world finally for all who choose to listen: I Love YOU... and I choose ONLY YOU!

You are my choice always.

6

You Deserve More

"But unto Hannah he gave a worthy portion; for he loved Hannah: but the LORD had shut up her womb."
1 Samuel 1:5

The thought of lavishing every desire fulfilled on the one you love is most of our dreams. The thought that we're able to supply whatever they desire would make any of us extremely satisfied. But that's not the way life is on most occasions.

For most of us, we have to choose what priority is at the moment while working towards the others. The majority of you who are reading this aren't millionaires who live in these super fancy and mega mansions (you might be getting there though). You're probably just people who are living the most abundant life as possible as you are working towards doing whatever you can to make the person you love the happiest possible.

In a perfect world, you have chosen the person that best suits where you are now, but they have something that reaches into your future seemingly making every dream you have since a child that much more of a possibility. They're filled with a level of understanding that far exceeds the rest of the individuals that you may have been in relationship with. They know what you can do and wait patiently while you work on the rest.

In spite of having a mate that is understanding and accepting it doesn't make you feel any less frustrated when you're not able to give them something that they really want. Especially, when you know that they've given you the best that they can without reservation. Maybe they were more successful when you met or maybe they were just wealthier. They met you at your lowest and for all of this time you've been eagerly desiring the day to give them what they've so freely given you.

You've seen them look in the magazines, drive pass those mansions and window shop for the finer things in life, but at this time you're just doing what you can with what you have.

Of course, those who are really connected to your heart understand this. They see your effort and know how hard you're working to make their lives enjoyable. You quietly accept their appreciation, but don't cease in your attempts to somehow fill the void that they may be experiencing.

The fact of the matter is that sometimes we just won't have to give what others want. With all of our best efforts we won't be able to supply what we know they desire. It's a hard pill to swallow, but it's the reality that most of us live in.

Sometimes the desire in our loves heart isn't anything physical that has anything tied to what we can do personally. Sometimes it's something that they just need to happen for them. Whether it's regarding their profession, education, family, friend or etc. Sometimes it's not even something that you can do. But this doesn't stop you from wanting to make it better.

No one wants to see the person that they love long for something that they can't fulfill. We would rather not look helplessly observing their pain than to watch them suffer the inconvenience of not having what their heart really desires.

So, in our meager attempts we do what we can to take the focus off of the void. It's important to note that sometimes our attempts might not look like they are well placed. Individuals might look at the "extra" and feel as though you are trying to make them forget about what they really need from you or a situation. Such was the story of Elkanah and Hannah.

Elkanah's ability to produce children was obvious. He had children by his other wife and they were growing, thriving and happy. But for some reason, what he was able to do for others, he was not able to do for her. Our ability to provide what other need are situation specific. It's quite possible to have provided something in one relationship, but because of various differences in time, individuality or financial status not be able to provide it currently. This can look kind of strange especially to the person at the other end of this relationship. You might hear things like, "Well, You did it for them". So, here you are now attempting to replicate a previous situation that has nothing to do with your desire, but rather your circumstance.

You can probably guess how this made Hannah feel to watch on the sidelines as Elkanah's other wife Peninnah's children grew. With every laugh, jump or cry it reminded Hannah of the joy of motherhood that she longed to have, but couldn't. I'm sure that she must've felt forgotten, but she wasn't. Elkanah loved her more.

In response to that love, he gives her more than he gave the others and I'm sure that they saw it. What the others failed to realize is that there really is no substitute for real like. The material things are just added benefits, but in the absence of those things it's absolutely love that matters. They had the children. But Hannah had his heart.

What's important to see about this is that he gives what he can. He doesn't want to just give her love. He wants there to be something else that demonstrates that it's real. It doesn't replace what she really wanted, but he wanted to give something that he had the power to control. Men would rather provide a situation that they can control instead of offering a situation that might become unstable. So, it's sometimes better to wait and work rather than to give something that might be lost.

It's sometimes easy to gauge someone's love for you based on what they give or what they can't give for that matter. So, in those scenarios it's a good idea to evaluate a person's ability to do what you're asking or desiring. It wasn't that he didn't want to provide her with what she needed. He just didn't have the power to control when and how she received it.

There may be times when the person you love really wants to do something special for you, but for whatever reason they just can't. Showing them that it's alright only readies their engines for the next opportunity to do what is actually in their hearts. Take the time to show them through your behavior and actions that you recognize that they want to do it. I guarantee you that it might spark a level of healing in them concerning a situation that might be totally frustrating and frightening to them. Another additional thing that you can do is to purposely choose the lesser. I know this sounds crazy and sounds like you're setting, but there is no harm in not asking for what you know they don't have the ability to do. This is not about value (because you rightfully deserve the best). It's about understanding.

I'm sure that Hannah not having children bothered him as well. The idea of not being able to give your wife the child she really wants would haunt any man just as much as it did Hannah. These weren't the days when medical technology could test to see who had the issue. They simply had to trust in one another. Most likely, Elkanah might've started to question in his heart what had changed in him that in this situation he was not able to give her what she wanted so badly. The perspectives concerning this story are endless.

How much do you trust the person you love? Do you really believe that they'll do the best they can when given the opportunity? Most of you are saying yes! You know their heart towards you and how much they're looking forward to making you happy. So, what can you do to make them secure in not being able to give you what they know you want? What can you do to demonstrate that you understand their desire and how you're willing to wait until the circumstances become more feasible?

Here's the awesome part. Hannah didn't become bitter towards him accusing him of attempting to make her forget what she desired, but rather she chose to pray. She redirects her passion towards the source of her fruitfulness. Elkanah could only do what he could, but she remembered a God who could do much more. You can call it the power of a praying woman or the beauty of God's timing. But whatever it was it worked.

Above everything, I believe that Elkanah really wanted Hannah to know how much she was loved. It didn't matter whether she had ten children or none. He didn't choose her because of that he chose her for who she was to him. Realizing why you've been chosen will help you during seasons where it seems like you can't have what you really want.

WHAT HE NEEDS YOU TO KNOW:

- You supply more in less than others can in much.
- He sees what your heart hides and is making plans to give it to you.
- He gives you more not to replace your desire, but because he loves you.
- There is no comparison. You are what he needs and wants.
- He wants to give you as much and more than you've given him.
- He needs your patience and understanding as he works to make it better for you.

There's no comparison to my love for you. In a world where may are lovely, beautiful and kind. You by far surpass them all.

How unlikely it would be for me to love you any less! It doesn't matter how much or how little you're able to give. It's always enough for me.

My heart, you deserve a whole lot more!

You deserve a lot more love, care, and kindness than any man can give you, sweetheart. If I were God, I'd recreate so many things of this world just for you... custom built I would suit your every need and desire. The thought of seeing your face smile with joy and happiness is my greatest desire. You truly deserve so much more.

You make my day every time you smile with those sweet, loving eyes holding me tight in mild clutches of loving warmth.

I would gladly give the whole world in exchange for the chance to fulfill your heart's desire. My heart too prays that one day this will become the reality we share together as we steadfastly enjoy the rest of our days.

Without even trying; effortlessly my love, you make up for all that (for now) you may seem to lack. Your presence in my life has brought more peace and love that I could have ever imagined.

I couldn't love you any lesser, with or without, you'll forever remain my only heartbeat... the light of my life... the love that gave me life afresh. I love you and no one can change that, not ever!

I want to give you so much more... I want to tour the world and buy you every rare gem I can lay hands on, I don't care the price to pay because you're worth so much more than money can ever buy.

O, how much more I desire to give you my love?! You simply deserve far much more!

I love you. With all my heart.

7

You're Worth the Wait!

"And it came to pass, that in the morning, behold, it was Leah: and he said to Laban, What is this thou hast done unto me? Did not I serve with thee for Rachel? Wherefore then hast thou beguiled me?

Genesis 29:25

One of the greatest days in history is the day that you finally find the one that you want to spend the rest of your lives with. It's kind of like all of the other days were foggy and without grandeur, but this day was brighter just because of them.

I can vividly remember the day that I saw my wife. I was at a special event sponsored by one of the church members in their home having a conversation with a colleague and I spot this lady walk by. I can remember what she was wearing as well. It was this black silk outfit or sorts. She walked by quickly and immediately I turn to my friend beginning to ask her questions concerning her. I wanted to know everything she knew about her. But she was not trying to give me any information for some reason. But I was not giving up.

The next day on a trip to Walterboro, SC as I was riding with other members on an engagement I blurted out to someone that I have found the person that I was going to marry. They looked back at me and smiled probably thinking that I had really lost my mind. Well, most likely to them I had. I was only nineteen years old. Didn't have a car, any money, my own place or anything. Yeah, it does sound kind of far-fetched, but isn't most love stories. You guys really don't believe that those soap operas are real right?

What's interesting about this story is that I have never spoken to her. Didn't have the nerve at the event where I first saw her and certainly didn't want to assume that she was available. I later found out that she was a little older than I was and more established that I was at that time. But I never doubted my ability to win her heart despite my lack of EVERYTHING.

As fate would have it I discovered something interesting. She attended the same church as I did and her mom loved me. How cool is this? I didn't even know that I was already in good with her family. The story only gets better. One day after service as we're exiting the building I finally muster up the courage to share with her my feelings and guess what? She was thinking the same thing.

To my amazement she was okay with me not having anything. I suppose she saw well beyond where I was and committed to help me get there. This was seventeen years ago!

WORKING WHILE YOU WAIT

The story of Jacob and Rachel is one of the most beautiful love stories of record in scripture. Jacob sees the beautiful daughter of Laban watering the flocks and is immediately smitten by her. In brave fashion, he assists her and wins her heart. What he could not have imagined is the lengths that he would have to go to in order to finally get her.

Can you remember the first time you saw the individual that you now love? What was the day like? Were your thoughts about them constant? You probably couldn't shake the idea of what your life could be like with them in it.

Jacob makes the first step in getting the attention of Rachel. He single handily removes the stone cover from off of the well demonstrating his strength and initiative. What we do know from the little we know about women (lol) is that they love men who make the first move. Most women aren't attracted to men who have to be pumped and pushed to pursue. You'll hear them from miles away screaming,

"He that findeth a wife finds a good thing". The operative and most pronounced word is "HE".

Rachel immediately sees this and returns to her father Laban's house with the report concerning this man. She's taken by his bravery and strength. He's won her heart. Over the next month they fall madly in love. Now this is where things get kind of tricky.

Jacob asks Rachel's father for his daughter in which her father gladly agrees. But unfortunately, it wasn't his intention to let Rachel the younger sister get married before Leah the oldest. Leah wasn't the most beautiful and was not even in Jacob's radar. The plot thickens.

Laban agrees to let his daughter go with one stipulation. Jacob had to work for him for seven years. I am not sure how many men would do the same today. We might work while we have her, but the idea of not having her and working might not go over too well. Unlike most of today's men, this was not a problem for Jacob.

Isn't it a wonderful dream to have someone see

so much of your value that they are willing to wait and work towards being with you for seven years. What about one year? To have someone see your worth to the put that they are willing to wait while you finish your education, make some more accomplishments or become financially stable would make anyone happy.

Now I want to mention that this patience is not just about women. Men too would love to have a women that is willing to wait on them. I've probably lost my entire female audience. A lot of the times we assume that a man doesn't want to settle down because he's some sort of player. But what if his desire to wait is to secure for you a more prosperous future? Would you be willing to wait then? Or would you choose another candidate who you think could give you want to want at that moment? Something to think about huh?

As the story would go on, Jacob works for Laban seven years. At the end of his agreement instead of getting the one he worked so hard for he was tricked and received Leah instead. Can you imagine the hurt he experienced? All of that work was seemingly for nothing. But in a twist of unparalleled passion he does something that I no one I know would do. He works another seven years with the promise of finally winning is first love.

The premise behind this chapter is to embrace the idea of patience as we are working towards not only providing things, but also strengthening love. Sometimes it's simply about how long and determined you can be to get who you really want. How much work are you willing to put into it? Are they worth it?

Finally, Rachel must have felt like the most special lady in the world. She knew that Jacob was committed to her from the beginning to whenever the end would come. Any man that would work for fourteen years to get you is definitely one that you can build something great with. She was worth the wait and the work. Her father didn't sell her cheaply. Even though his schemes weren't just he knew as a father what she was worth.

Just as Laban knew. Your heavenly father knows as well that you're value far exceeds what money or gifts can buy. You too are worth it. Choose today to Accept, Acknowledge and Honor yourself as the gift to the one who is willing to work and wait.

WHAT HE NEEDS YOU TO KNOW:

- I take pleasure in being brave for you.
- You don't have to worry about rushing for me. I see your value and am willing to wait for you.
- Give me the opportunity to work for you. My energy and effort belong to you.
- Your value far exceeds what money can buy. You are my gift and I'll always treasure you.

Minute after minute, as the hours drag by, day after day, I work hard for a prize far beyond any worth of silver or gold.

Day by day, I look up into the sky... I watch the birds fly by, I see the clouds gently floating by. They pass over my weary head, my shoulders display hard muscles from years of strong engagement in an effort to attain the goal that lies just at my arm's reach, yet only time may eventually grant me the fulfilment of my most sincere heart's desire – the beauty of your life intertwined with mine.

I would like to let you know, therefore, my love, that you indeed are worth the wait. You are worth every single moment that I spend, forging on closer, slowly yet ever surely toward my mark.

Here I am, here I stand patiently… darling, I give myself away as a living sacrifice for the unfailing purpose of securing your love and a befitting life with you beside me my dear precious wife, worthy indeed of every acclaim.

You are worth every little drop of sweat, of tears, of hope of a better, brighter tomorrow because without you in my life there really is no essence. Vain shall be the sheer intents of many on the outside our camp who plot in secret to make a nuance out of my long nurtured quest of love that, in the end, only love shall speak. Love that gives me the undying strength to press harder, stronger with only you in my view.

I will give my all just to have you. No matter

what great gap stands between to stop me from reaching and taking that which is rightfully mine as it is written, 'the laborer is worthy of his wages'.

Every day turns into night, my eyes ever void of weakness, hope keeping me strong, never fainting with the light that a glorious future with you sheds upon my heart... I muse at the futile attempts of others to hold me back for, patiently I will persevere until the day that I finally take hold of my worthy prize – You!

Silver and gold, even the gold of Ophir, precious rubies and all nature of colorful beautiful diamonds vainly add up to the beauty and wonderful breath of sheer joy and fulfillment you so freely pour forth into my life. I will stand right here, outside the courts of your tent, feet buried deep in the earth of time, waiting, praying, announcing my unending love as I anticipate the release and installation of my true heart's desire.

I have sworn and I will not relent, you are

worth the wait and I don't care what it takes; an eye or a limb, as long as your love for me abounds I will stand eternally strong keeping in clear sight that final moment when you and I will exhale with long-awaited relief and joy.

You are definitely worth it, my dear. I will wait for all time if I have to… and I will do so because you are indeed a worthy goal to attain at the irrecoverable expense of time.

Simply said, Sweetie… you are worth the wait! And I love you forever!

I'm yours…

Made in the USA
Columbia, SC
14 June 2023

18063751R00071